Dot-to-Dot

NATURAL WORLD

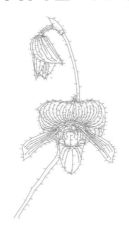

Dot-to-Dot

NATURAL WORLD

Join the dots to discover fascinating scenes from nature

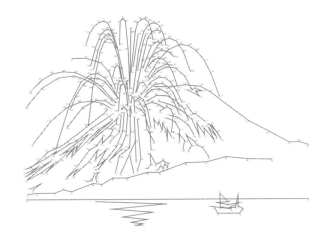

Glyn Bridgewater

southwater

Introduction

Dot-to-dot puzzles have long been a popular activity for young and old alike with the opportunity to happily while away the hours uncovering hidden scenes lying amongst the dots. This challenging new book takes simple join the dot art to the next level with 40 puzzles of birds, wild animals, flowers and natural phenomena around the world. Intricate, challenging and rewarding to finish, the puzzles range from 258 to 1324 dots and will have you transfixed as you progress from dot to dot trying to see what image materializes.

An absorbing and relaxing activity that can calm and reduce daily stresses and anxieties, these brain-stimulating puzzles can contribute to alertness. There are also proven educational benefits to doing a dot-to-dot activity. It helps to build fine motor skills, improve concentration levels and strengthen mapping skills – all while creating memorable art to enjoy. Each drawing may take approximately half an hour to complete, perfect for a rainy day or holiday activity, or simply a chance to take yourself away for some peace and quiet for a while.

Among the amazing scenes from nature included here are a golden eagle in full flight, dramatic icebergs in Antarctica, a dragonfly hovering over a water lily, an exotic sunset in Hawaii, and many more. They are all beautiful examples of nature's flora and fauna and have been photographed or painted very many times by enthusiastic naturalists.

These fascinating natural scenes have been 'captured' as dot-to-dot puzzles, their identities waiting patiently to emerge from the depth of the dots to reveal what they are.

As some of the drawings are quite intricate in parts it is best to use a pen (rather than a pencil) with a fine tip. Starting at number 1, connect the dots in numerical order. If a number is next to a circle rather than a dot, lift your pen and start again at the next consecutive number. This number may not necessarily be close to the previous number, it can be anywhere on the design.

Continue completing the picture in this manner, picking up your pen whenever you come to a circle until you have come to the last dot. For the most accurate picture, try to keep a relatively straight line between the connecting dots, but don't worry if you make a mistake or have a wobbly line, it won't affect the finished piece.

Once you have completed your dot-to-dot artwork, turn to the back of the book where you can compare your work with the finished solution and also read some interesting facts about the image you have drawn.

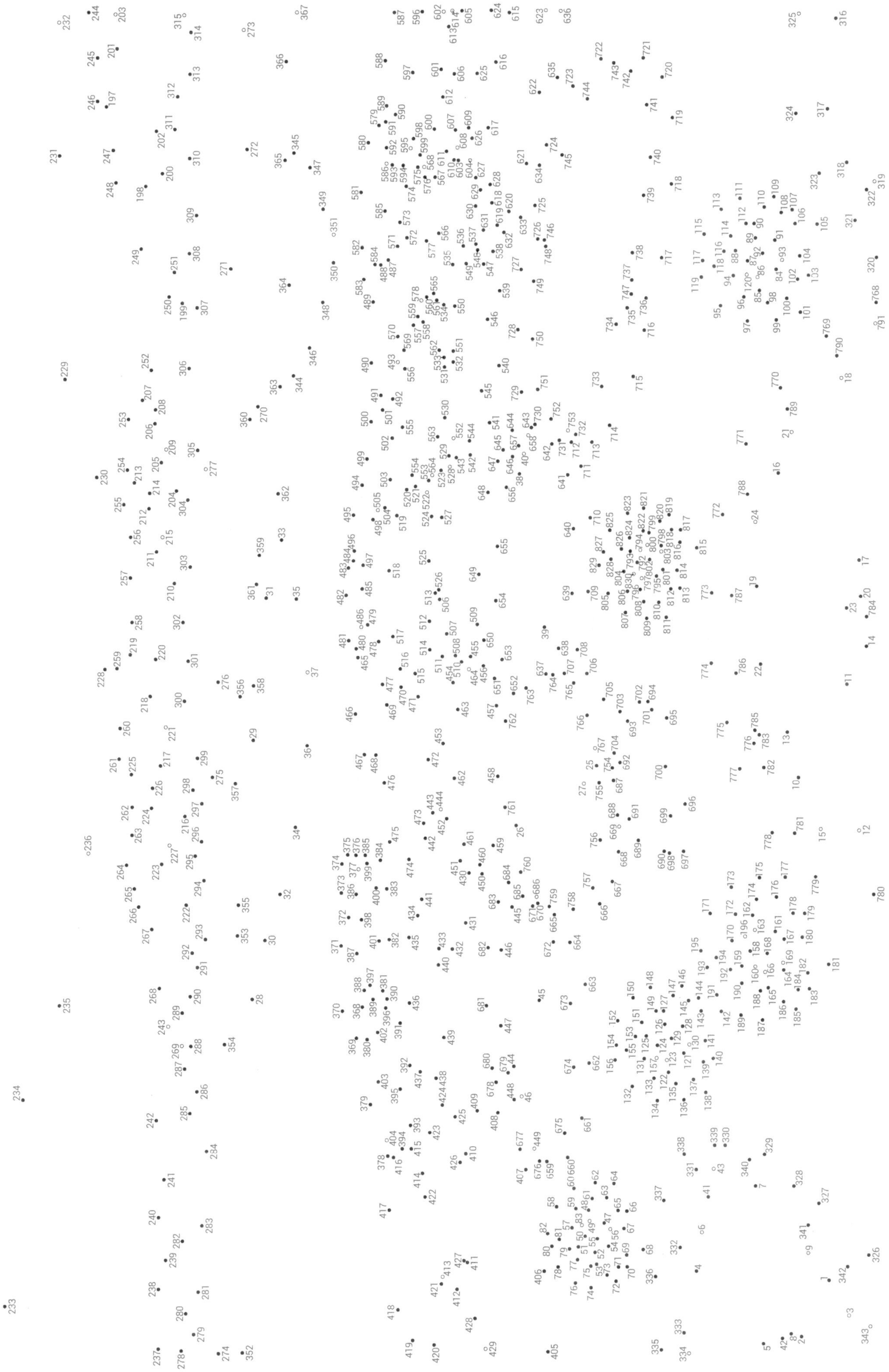

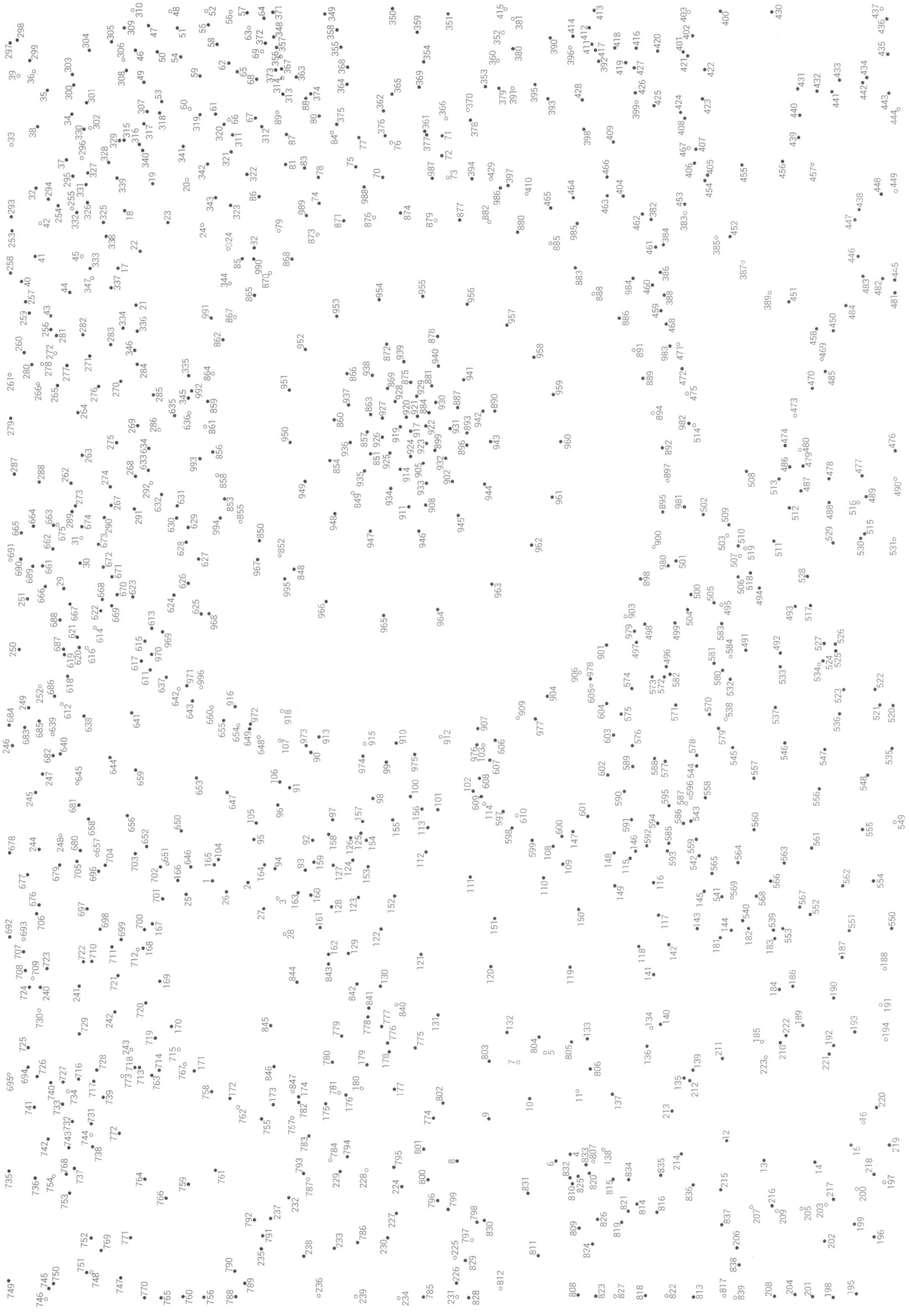

5

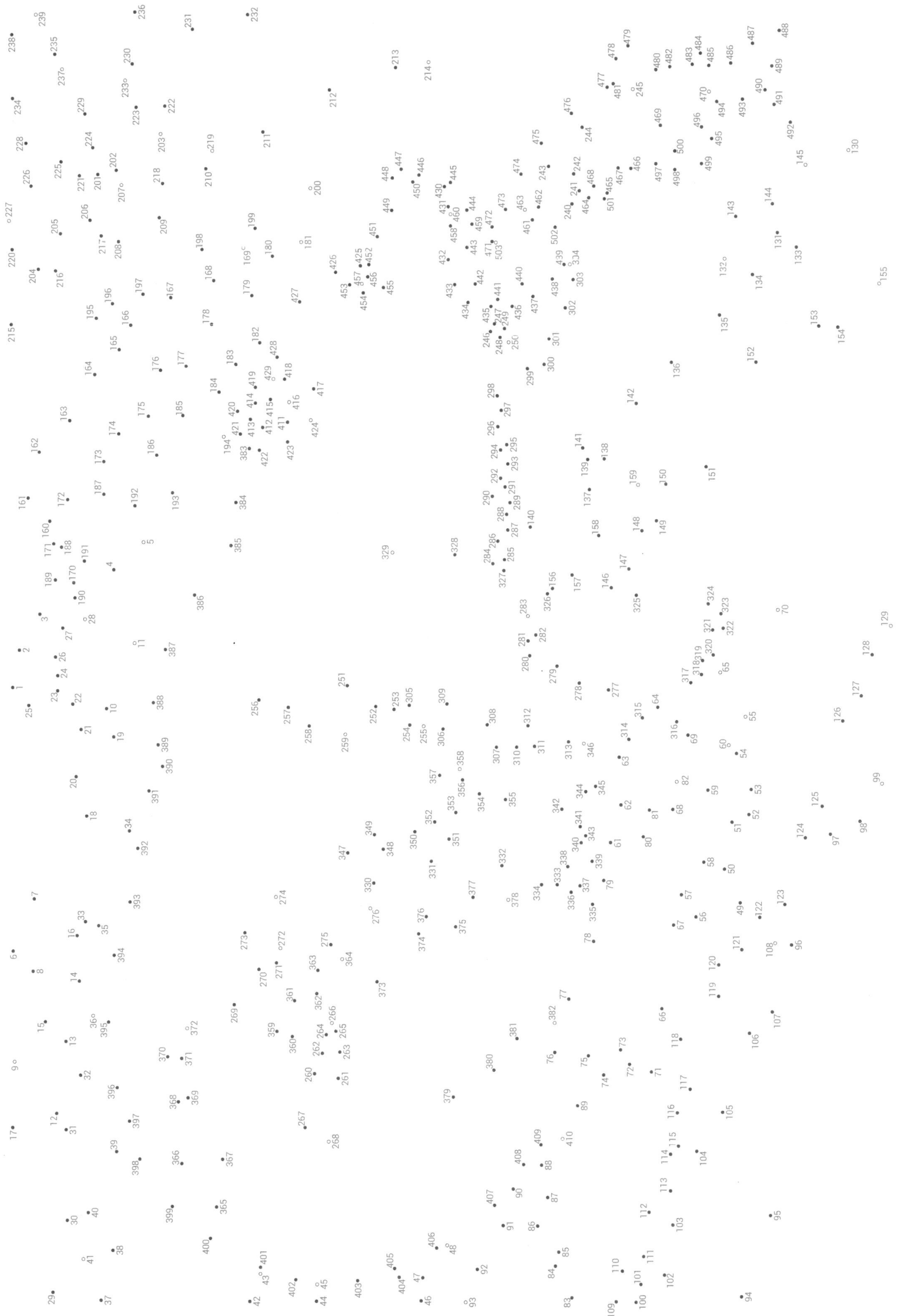

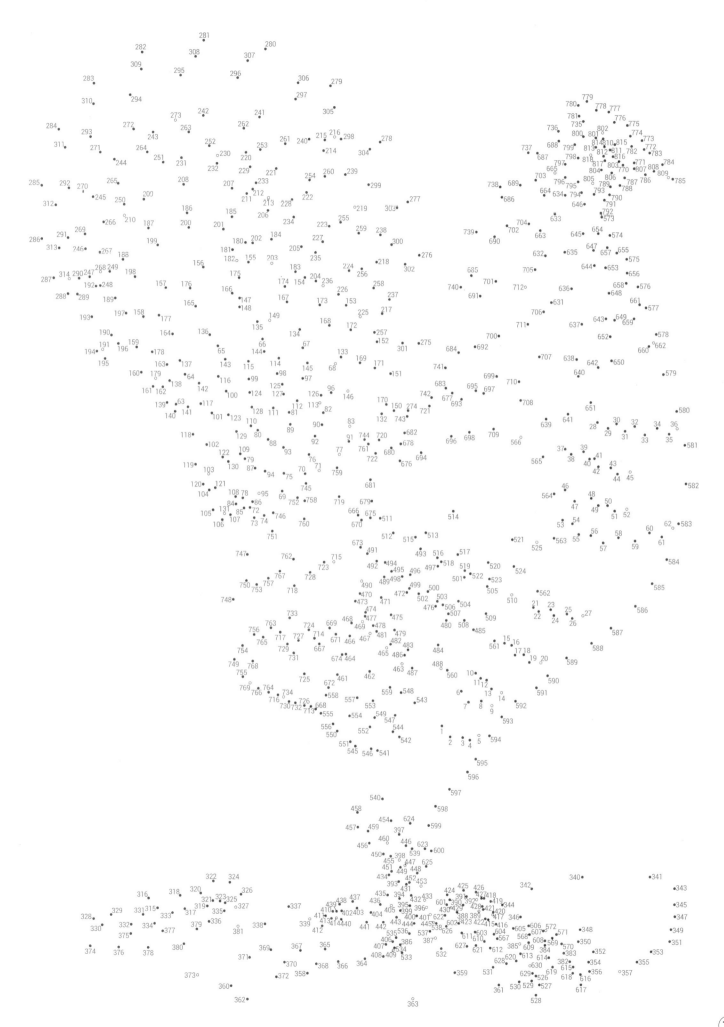

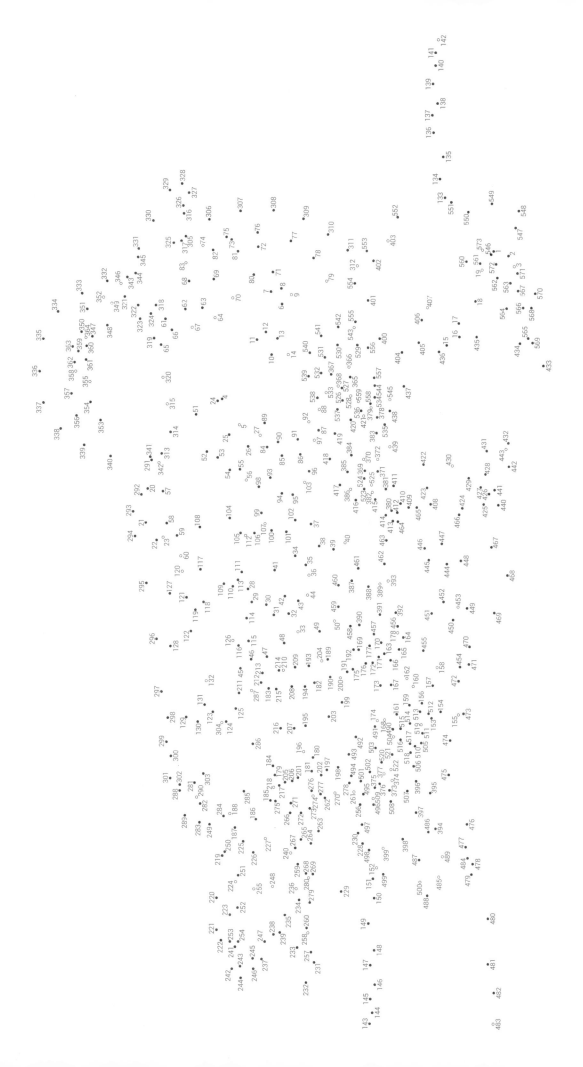

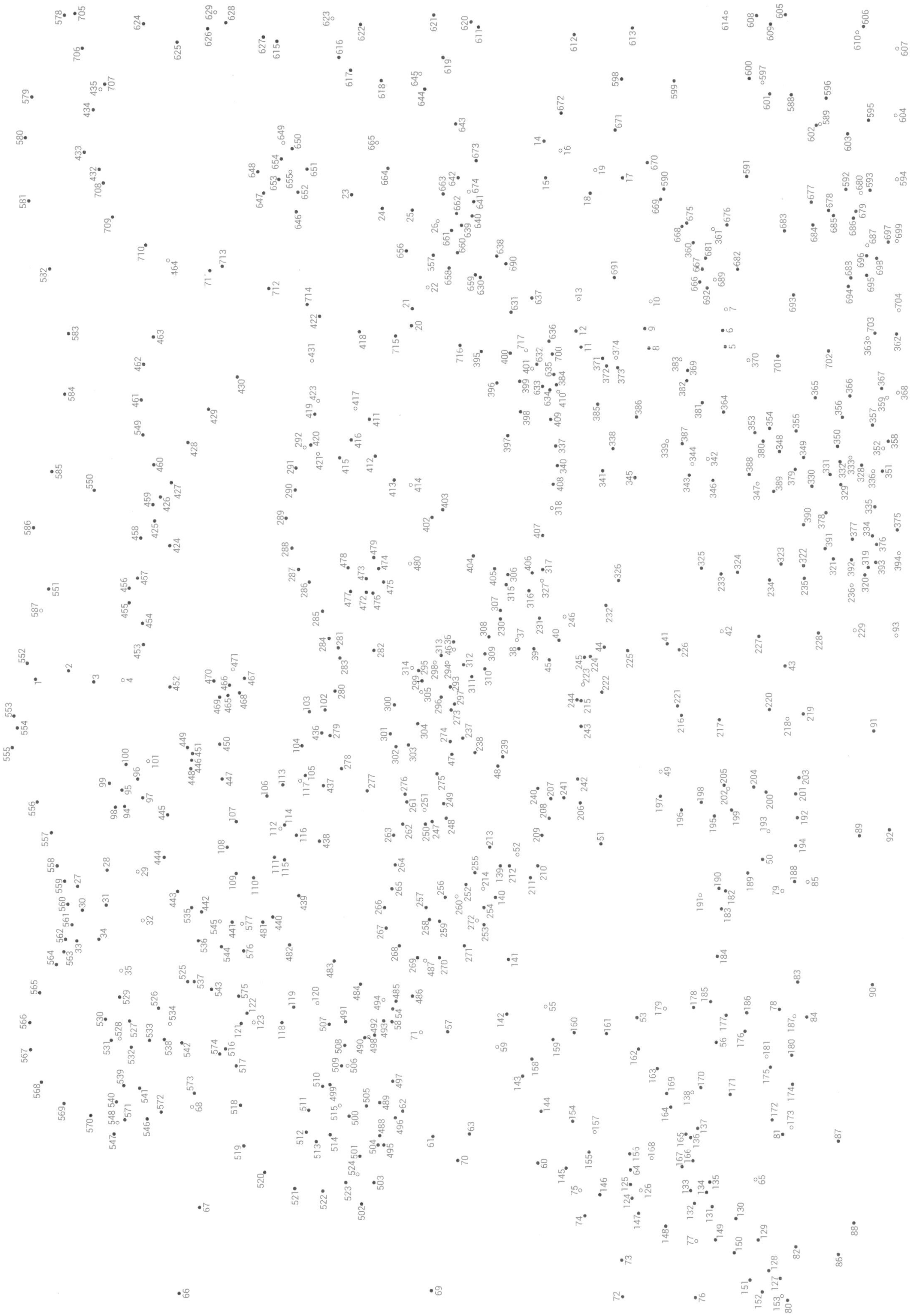

18

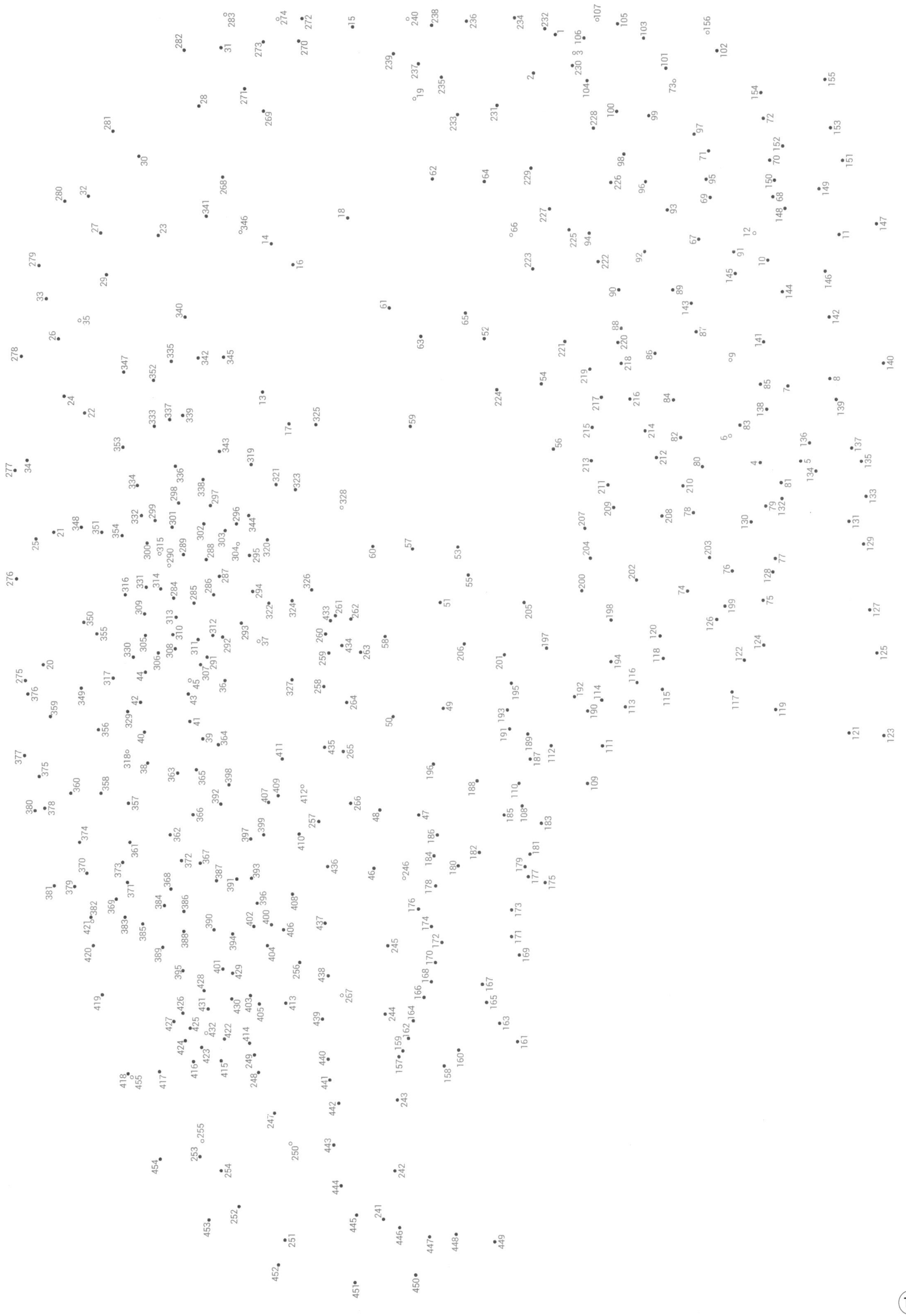

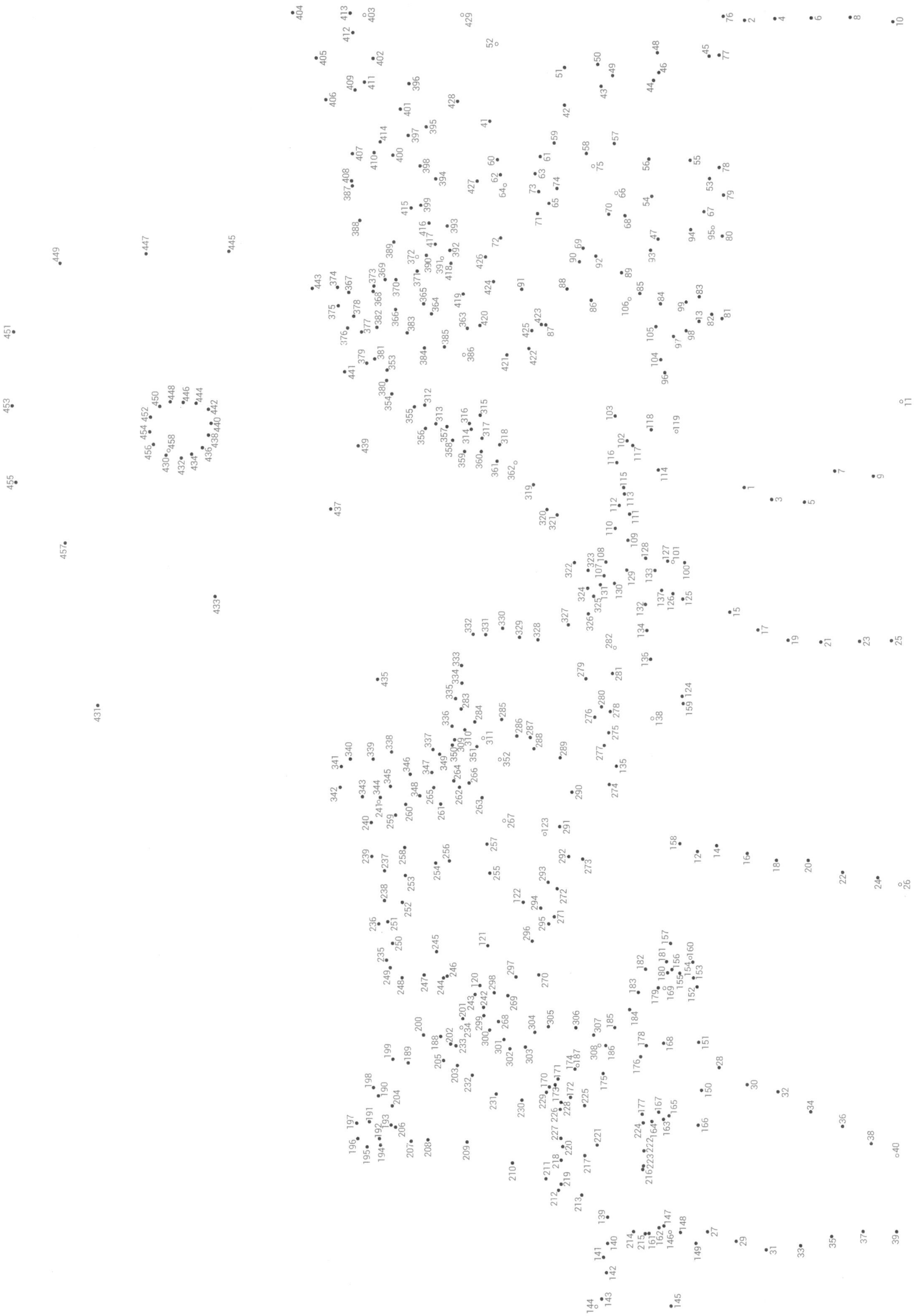

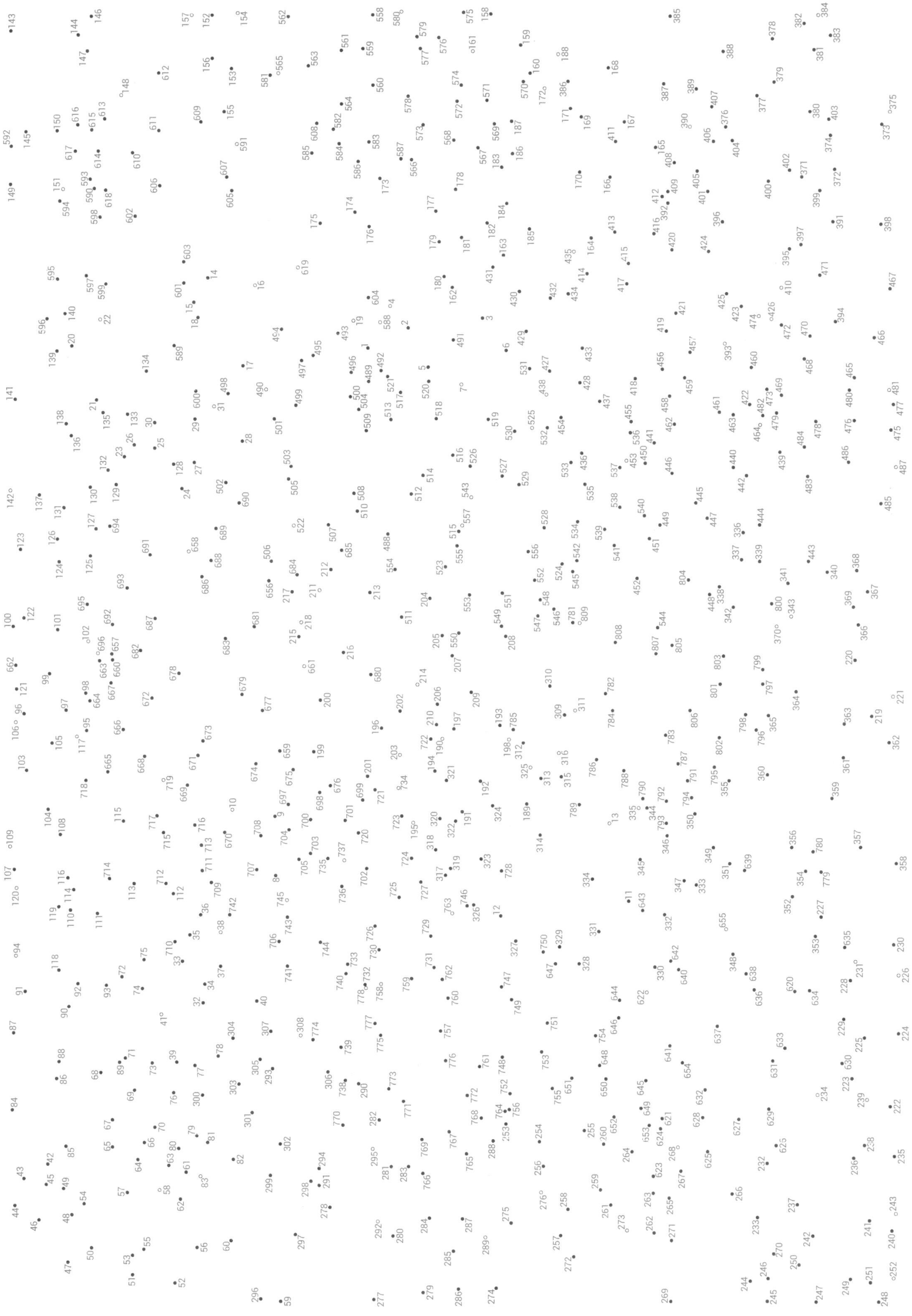

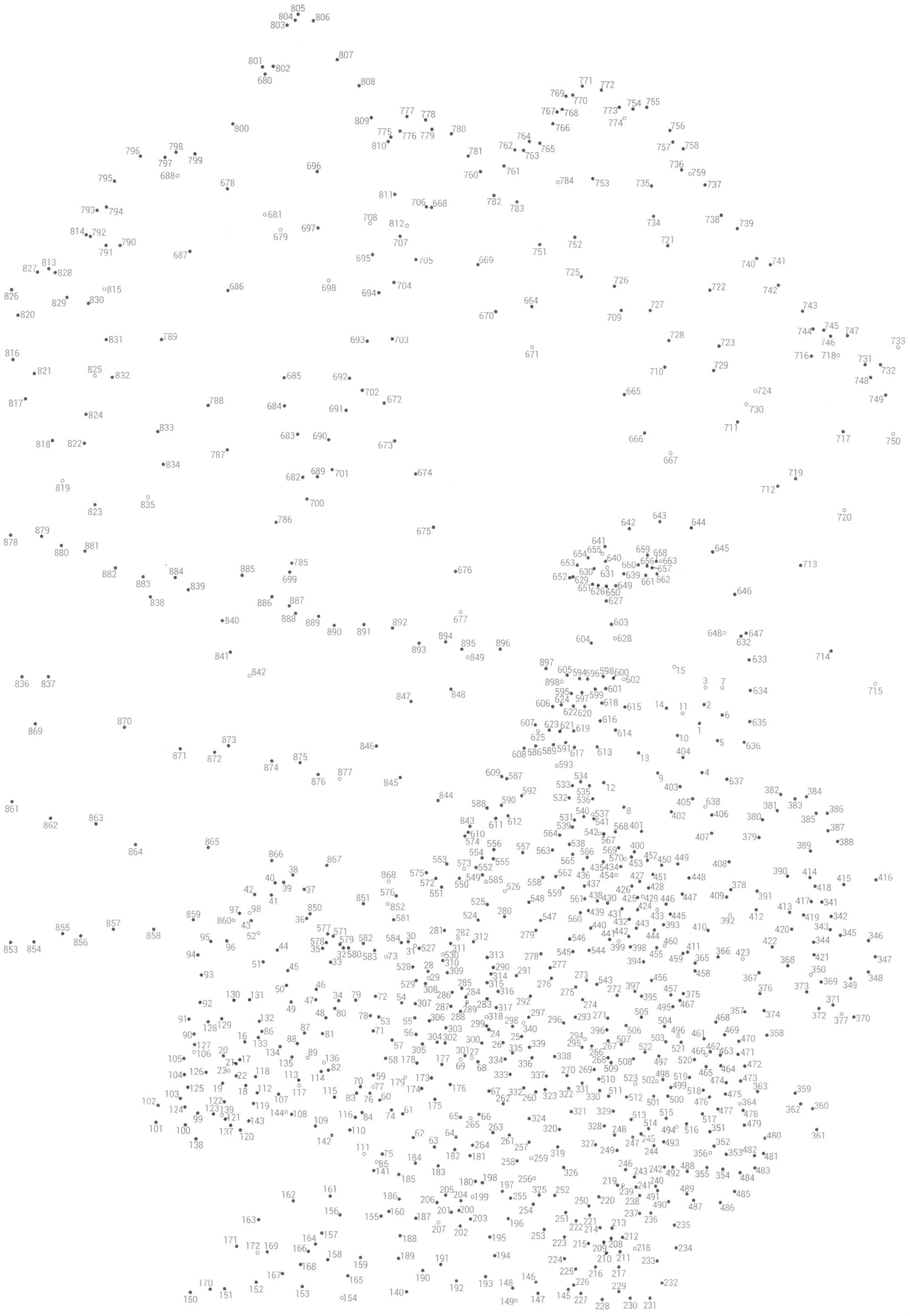

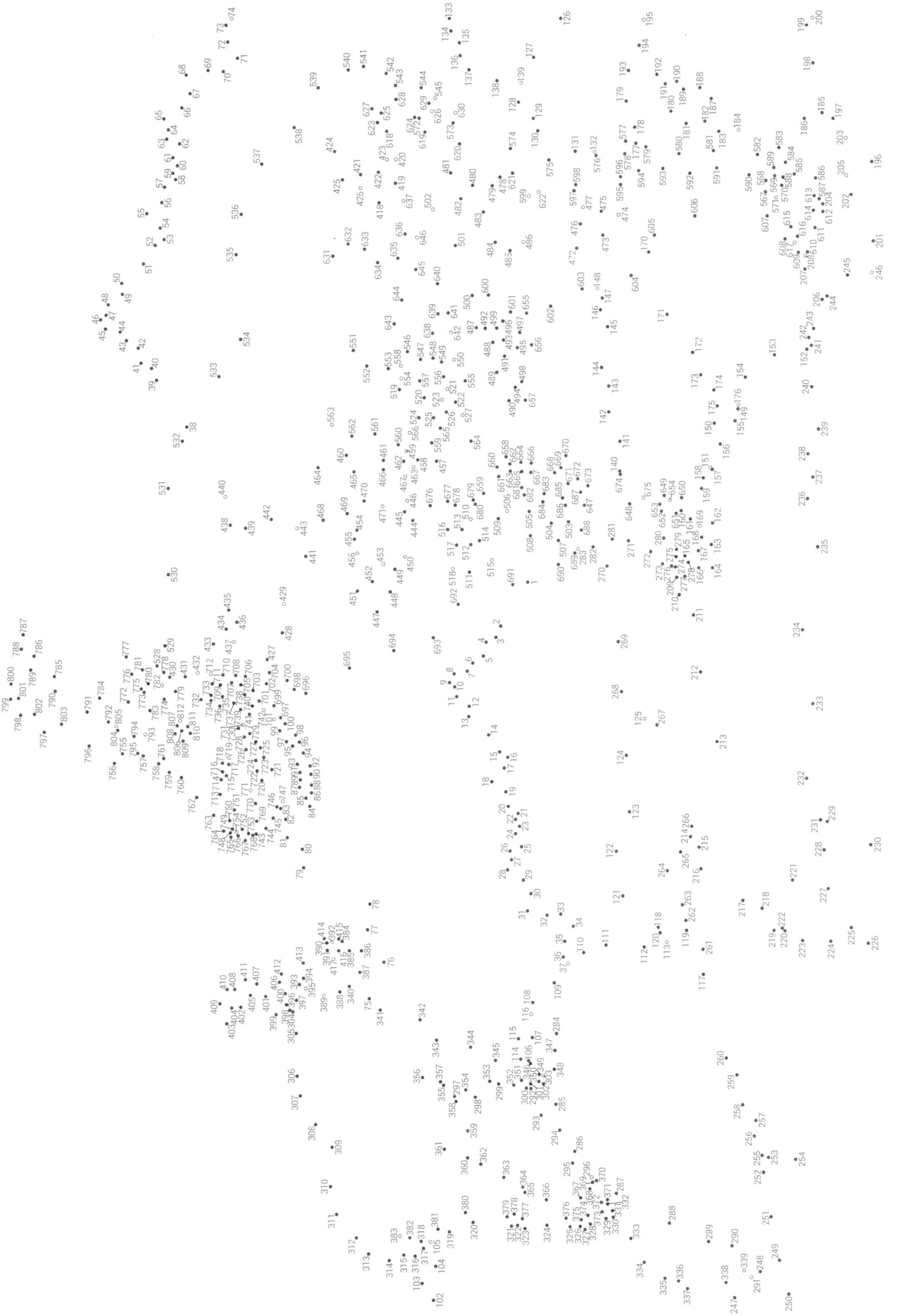

28

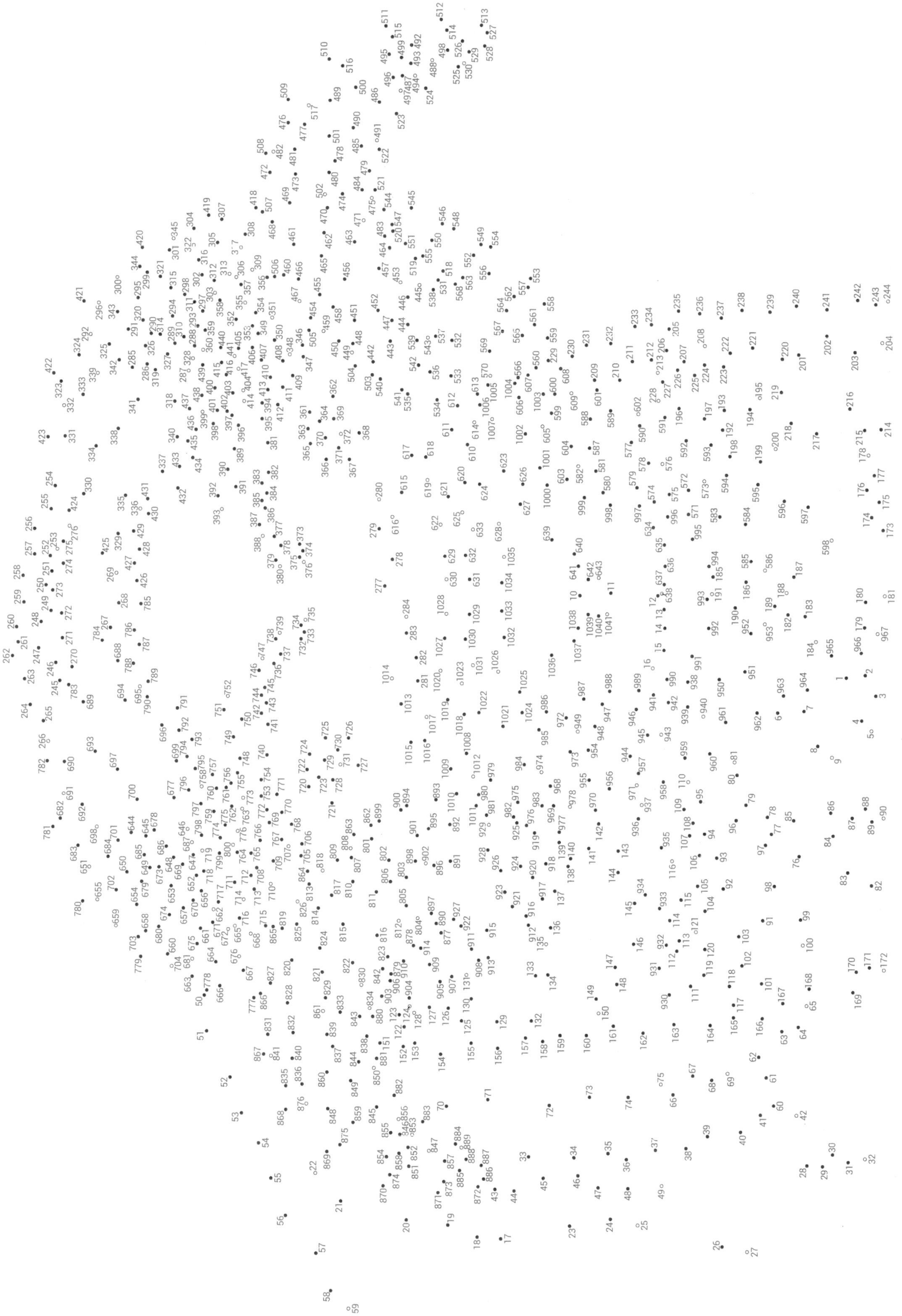

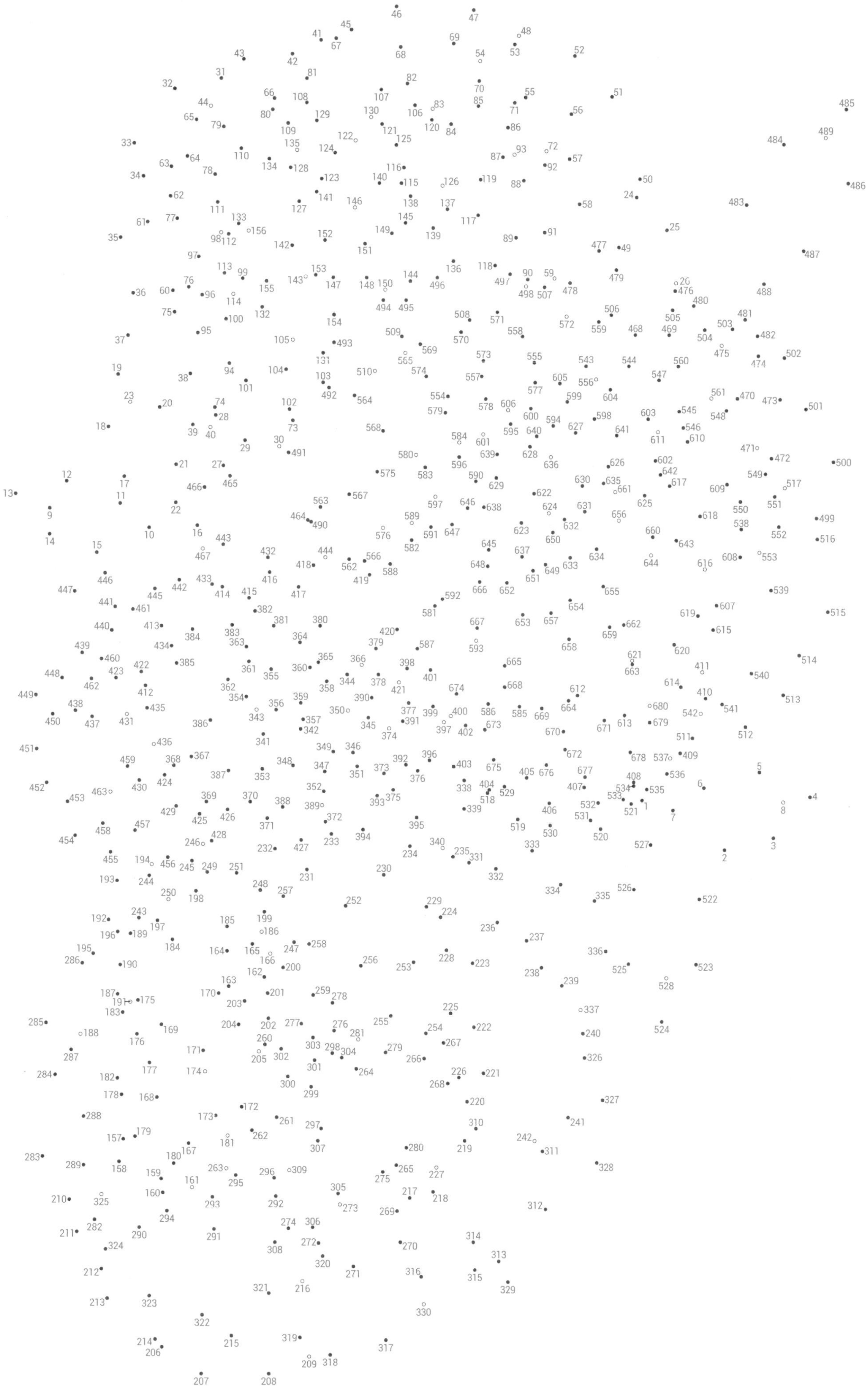

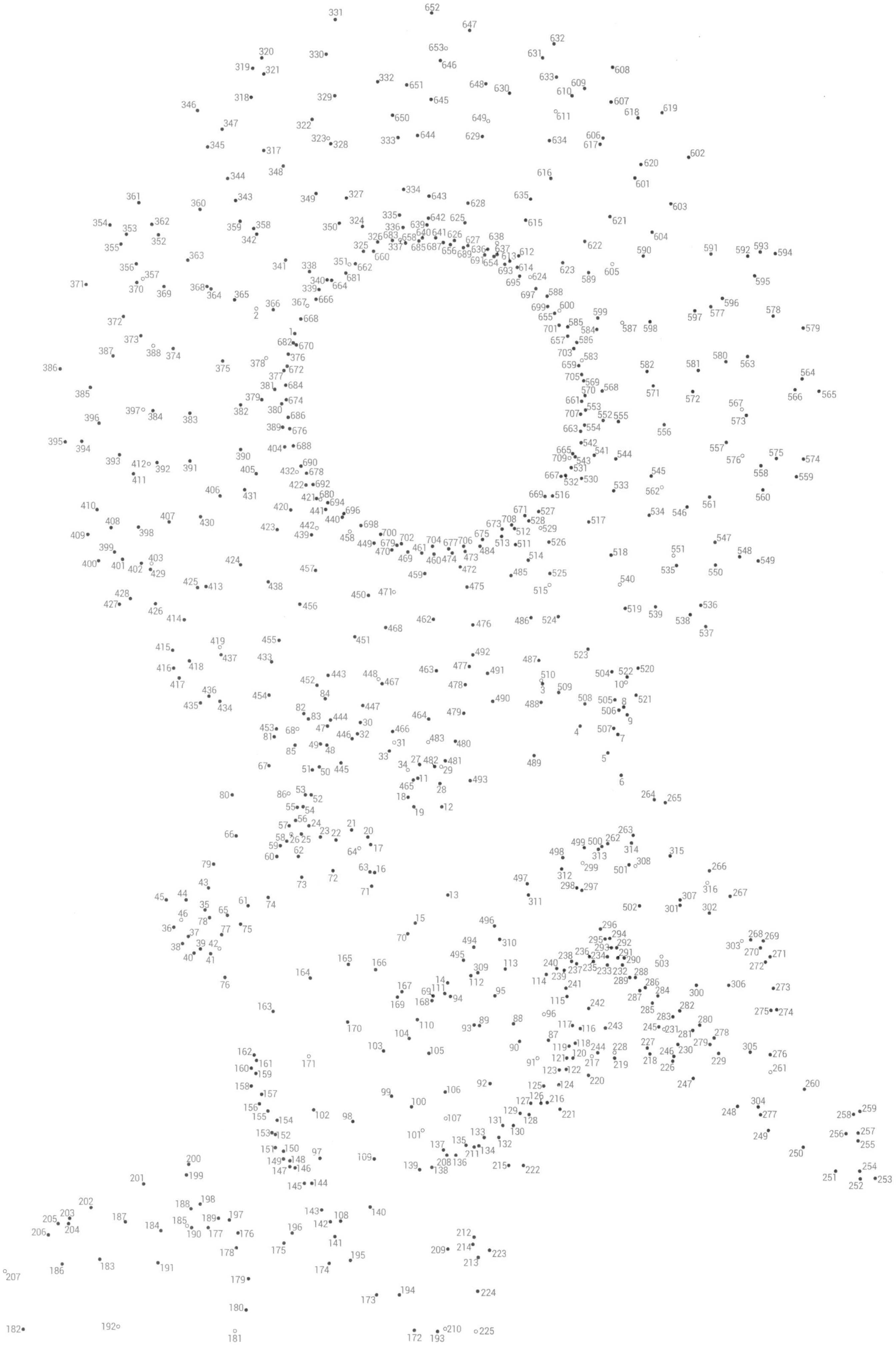

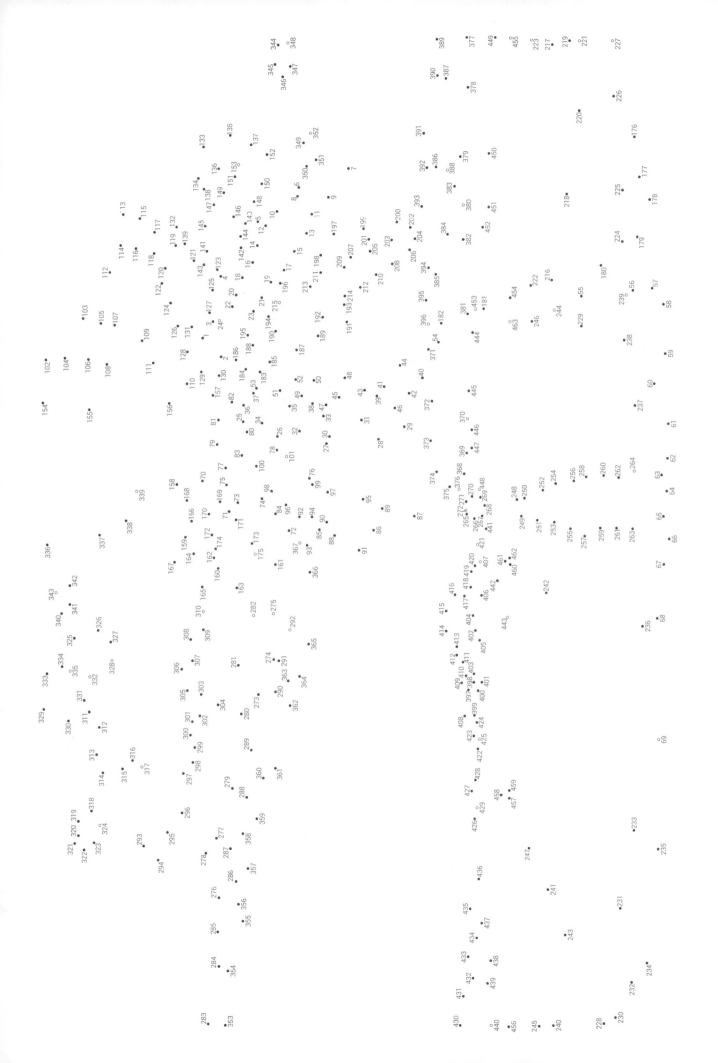

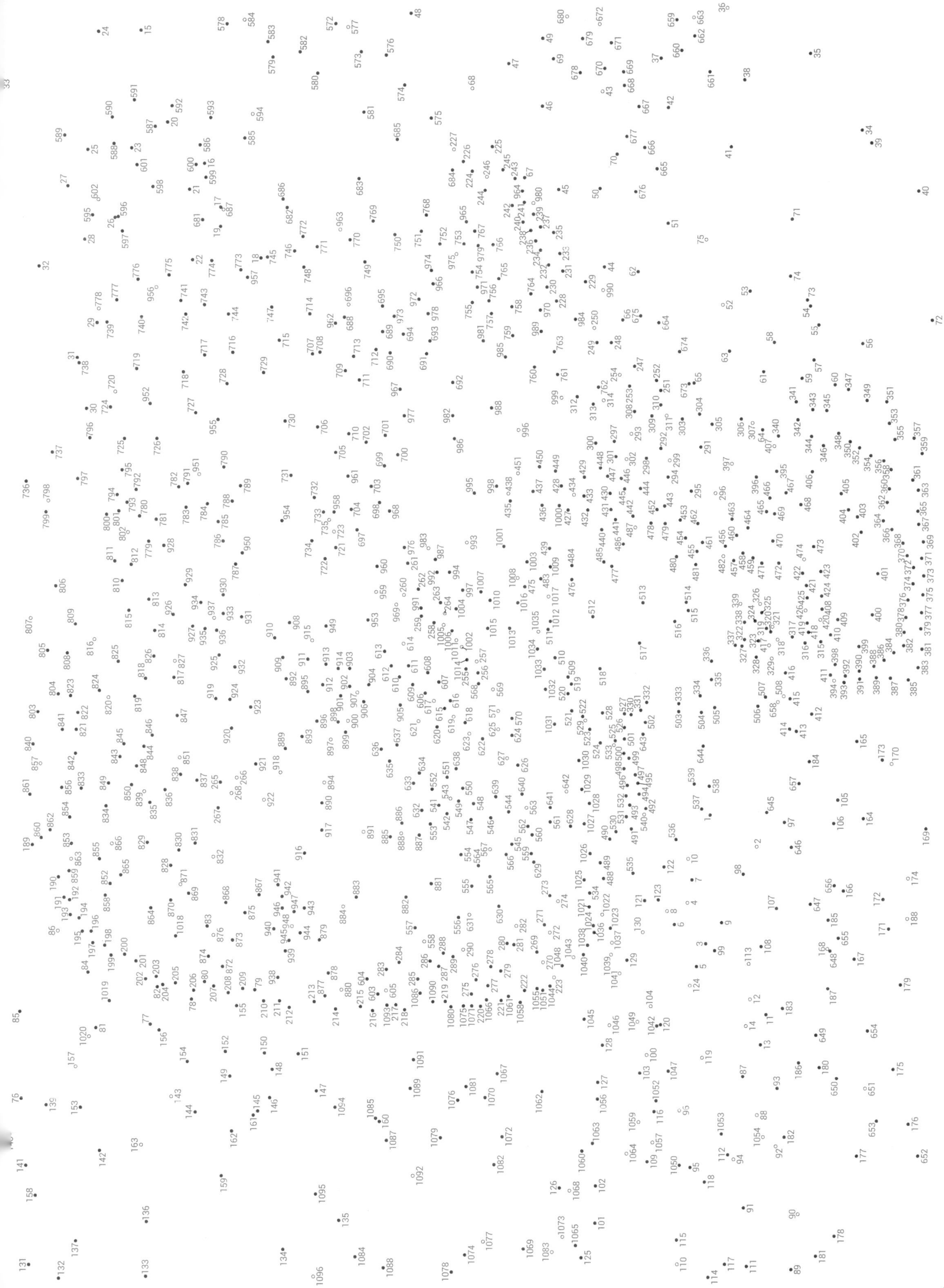

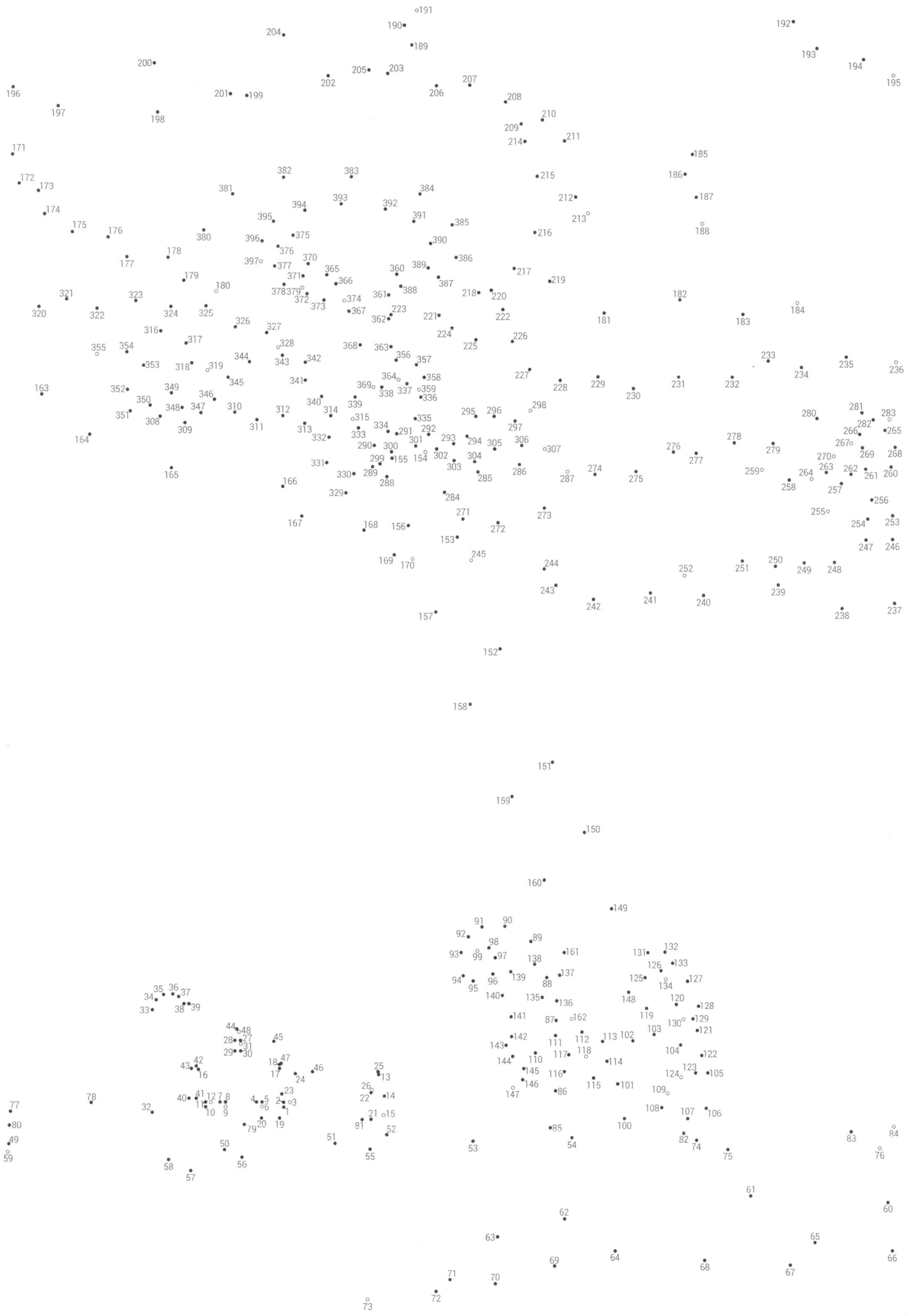

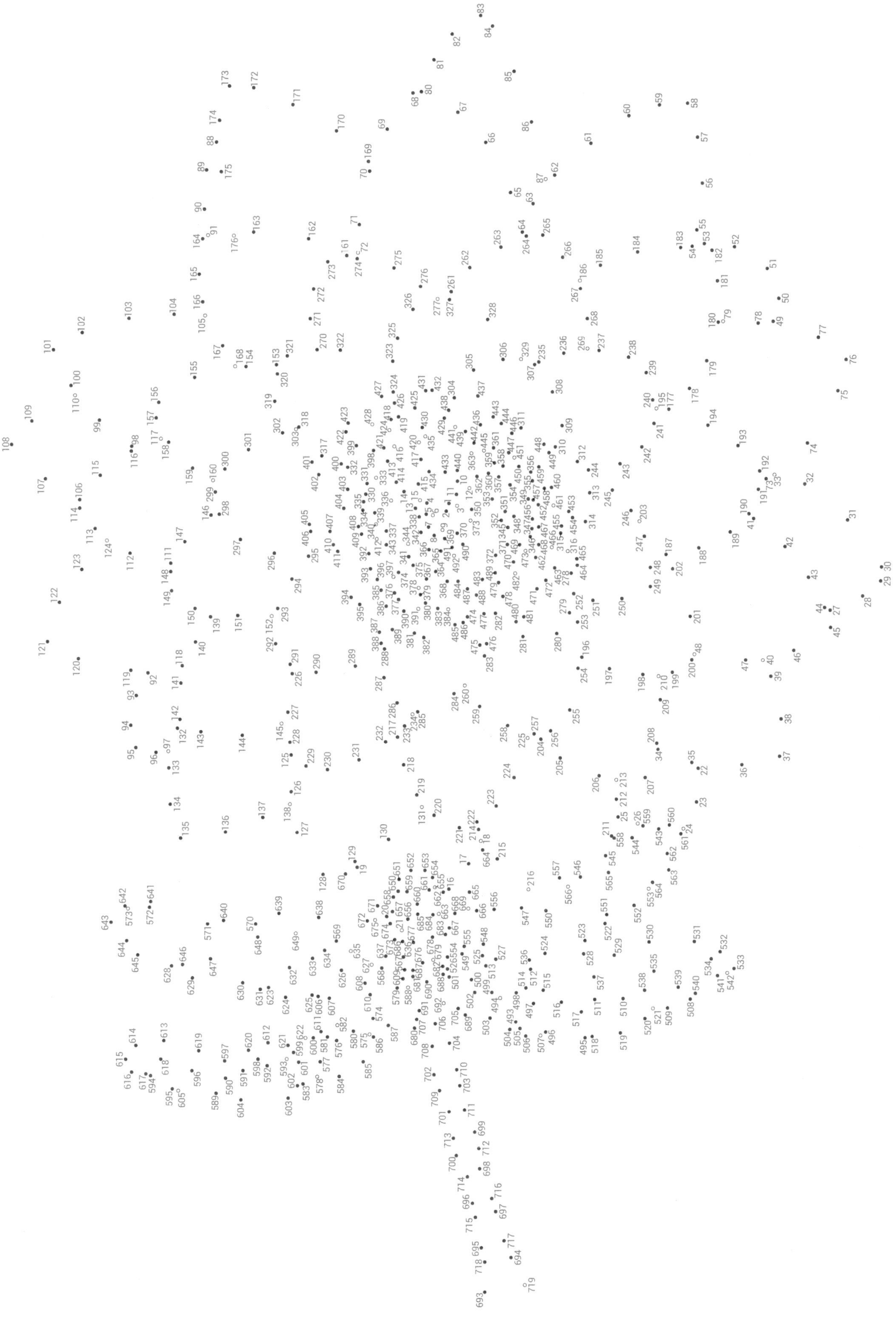

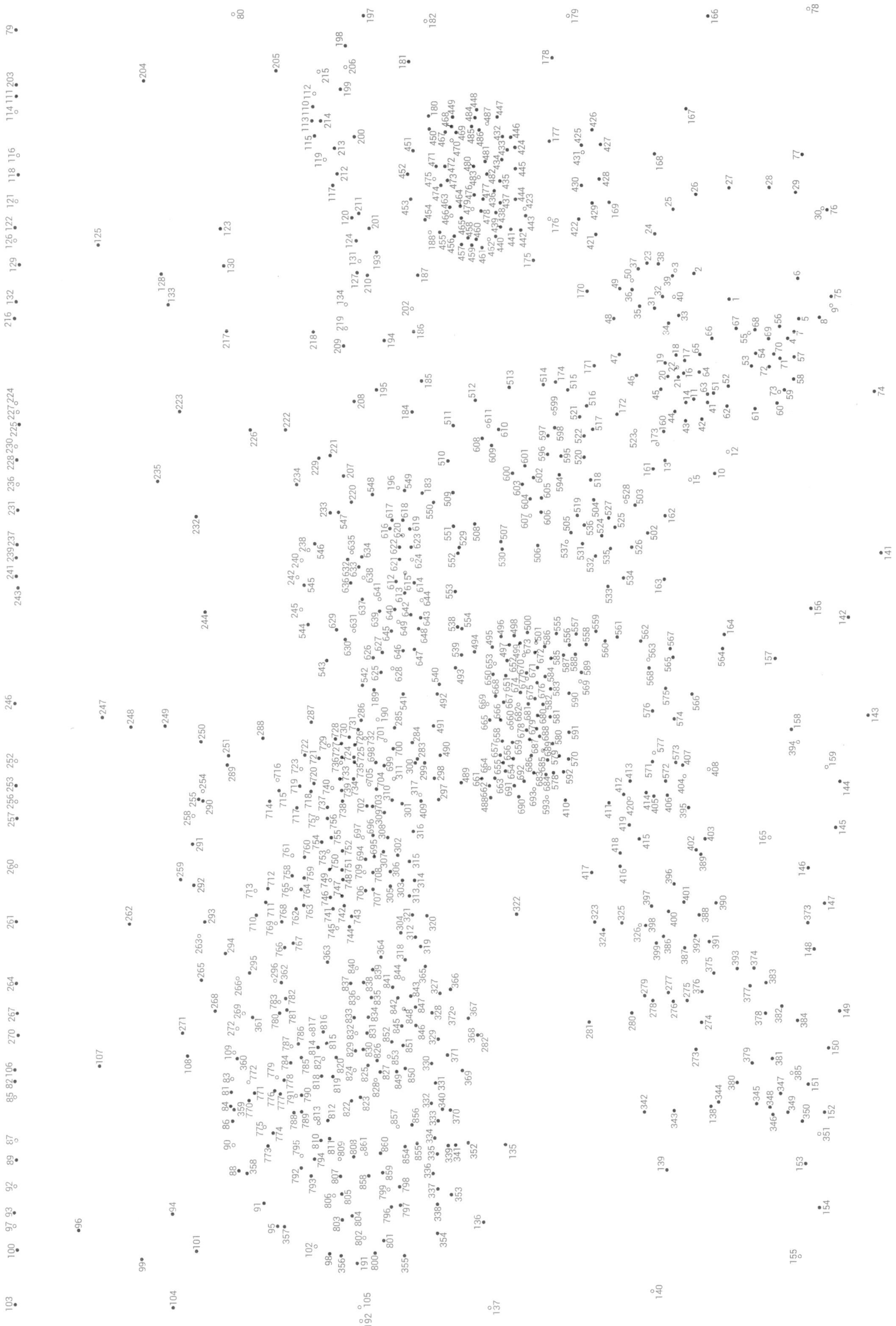

Page 1

Alpine Mountains

The Alps form the largest mountain range in Europe, stretching in the shape of a crescent arch, from Austria and Slovenia in the east all the way through Italy, Switzerland and Germany to France in the west. It is home to many glaciers and its highest peak is Mont Blanc in France, standing at 4,810m/15,782ft. There are 13,000 species of vegetation and 30,000 species of wildlife in the Alps, many of which are native to the region. **509 dots**

Page 2

Amazon River

Located in South America, the river is approximately 6,400km/4,000miles long and runs through Guyana, Ecuador, Venezuela, Bolivia, Brazil, Colombia and Peru. Teeming with wildlife, there are over 3,000 known species of fish living in the Amazon river, including the meat-eating piranha and the arapaima, the second-largest freshwater fish in the world. **830 dots**

Page 3

Ammonite and Shells

Seashells are created by animals that live in the sea. The shell itself was part of the body of the creature, which has since died, and the soft inner parts have been eaten by other fish or have rotted out. Ammonites, with their distinctive ribbed spiral-form shell, are perhaps the most widely known fossils. The creatures that created these shells lived in the seas between 240–65 million years ago. **996 dots**

Page 4

Anemone and Clownfish

The star of the movies 'Finding Nemo' and 'Finding Dory', the clownfish is a well-recognized marine fish. Also called false clownfish, they live in the coral reefs around Australia and Southeast Asia. Their natural habitat is certain types of anemones (a creature that anchors itself to the sea floor and uses its tentacles to attract food). Clownfish are orange with three white bands, edged with black on the head and body. **905 dots**

Page 5

Arizona Desert Cactus

The saguaro cactus grows exclusively in the Sonaran Desert, which spreads from the southwestern United States of Arizona and California into northwestern Mexico. These distinctive plants are large, tree-like columnar cacti that develop branches (or arms) as they age, although some never grow arms at all. They are incredibly slow-growing – a saguaro is usually 50–70 years old before it grows its first branch. **447 dots**

Page 6

Bear Hunting Fish

During the fall, salmon migrate from the ocean to the upper reaches of their native rivers to breed. Brown and grizzly bears take advantage of this annual event to feast on the migrating fish. Skilled predators, the bears spend several hours in the water intercepting the salmon. It is estimated that during the few weeks of the salmon run a grizzly bear takes on nearly 90% of its annual energy needs. **503 dots**

Page 7

Bird Feeding Young

Adult birds work extremely hard to feed their young while still in the nest. For the first few days the adult male or female will regurgitate food to make it easier to digest for the young. After that, they bring them whole food including bugs, caterpillars, worms and moths. Baby birds get their water from the food they are being fed. **557 dots**

Page 8

Blossom and Butterfly

Butterflies love feeding off flowers to sip their nectar. The flower has to be able to support the weight of the butterfly, and the butterfly's legs have to be able to latch onto the flower because butterflies don't hover while they feed. Butterflies can see a large spectrum of colour through their compound eyes, including ultraviolet, enabling them to see patterns in flowers that we can't see. **672 dots**

Page 9

Bromeliad

There are almost 3,000 members of the tropical plant family Bromeliaceae, including the pineapple. They are a popular plant for ornamental purposes because they are easy to grow and care for, and produce beautiful, long-lasting flowers. In the wild, the roots of the bromeliad do not form in the ground but grow on top of rocks and trees and are therefore known as 'air plants'. **652 dots**

Page 10

Cockerel

The striking plumage of the cockerel differentiates this male chicken from the female hens. It is also larger than the average hen with a bigger comb on the top of its head. A cockerel makes a very loud crowing sound, usually early in the morning although they can crow at anytime of the day. Its loud shrill is to ward off other roosters. **818 dots**

Page 11

Daffodils

As a harbinger of spring the daffodil is one of the best-loved of all bulbs, and many thousands of cultivars have been grown over the years. They are predominantly yellow but some species are white. There are about 50 species, originally growing in a wide range of habitats in Europe and North Africa where they are found in meadows and woodlands and even in rock crevices. **1324 dots**

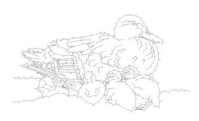

Page 12

Ducks

A diverse group of waterfowl, ducks can be distinguished by their relatively small size compared with swans and geese. They inhabit stretches of open water, though typically become more secretive when nesting. Drakes usually come into more vibrant plumage before the onset of the breeding season. A common sight in spring is a group of unpaired males chasing potential mates. **573 dots**

Page 13

Bald Eagle

Fish is the primary food of bald eagles, although they will also eat a variety of small mammals as well (the average eagle will eat around 600g/1lb of food a day). However, eagles do not need to eat every day; they have an area called 'the crop' to store food. Bald eagles make their large nests at the tops of old trees that are close to large areas of open water. **557 dots**

Page 14

Elephants Drinking

Elephants are very social animals that form deep family bonds and live in tight groups of related females. Male elephants tend to be solitary creatures. The elephant herd is led by the oldest, and often largest, female called the matriarch. A family unit can range from 3 to 25 individuals. Other family units also combine to become part of the main herd. Late in the evening, large numbers of elephants can be found congregating around a watering hole. **717 dots**

Page 15

Small Tree Finch

The small tree finch has a grasping bill that enables it to deftly pick up insects and caterpillars from the surface of bark and leaves, and to bite through the bark of twigs and leaf stems to reach insect larvae. Natives of the Galapagos Islands, they are one of the 13 species of finches Darwin studied while travelling around the Galapagos Islands and helped to support his theory of evolution. **623 dots**

Page 16

Coral Reef Fish

Coral reefs make up just 1 percent of the world's oceans and yet provide a home for 25 percent of all marine fish. Hundreds of species can exist in a small area of a healthy reef, many of them hidden or well camouflaged. Some species have evolved thin, flattened bodies that are effective in making sharp turns, enabling the fish to quickly manoeuvre out of danger. **686 dots**

Page 17

Flock of Geese

A flock of geese is also called a 'skein' of geese, and the sight of large swathes of Canadian geese flying down from the Great White North to overwinter in the mid to southern United States is a spectacular annual event. The geese fly in a large 'V' formation, with one bird in the lead and the others trailing behind in two diverging lines. Scientists believe that the reason they fly in a 'V' formation is to expend less energy on the wing, with each goose taking its turn at the front. **415 dots**

Page 18

Giraffe

Instantly recognized by its exceptionally long neck, the giraffe is the tallest living animal: an adult male stands 4.6–6m (15–19ft) tall. It also has the longest tail of any land mammal. Most giraffes live on the savannas, grasslands or open woodlands of East Africa, Angola and Zambia in southwestern Africa. Their diet consists of evergreen leaves during the dry season and deciduous new leaves once the rainy season begins. **771 dots**

Page 19

Golden Eagle

This formidable eagle is North America's largest bird of prey and the national bird of Mexico. They are extremely fast and can dive upon their quarry at speeds of more than 240km/150miles per hour. They use their speed and sharp talons to snatch up rabbits and squirrels. Golden eagles mate for life and make their nests in high places, such as cliffs, trees or tall man-made structures such as church spires or towers. **455 dots**

Page 20

Wild Horses

While most horses are domestic, others remain wild, or feral, in certain environments around the world, notably the United States of America, Scotland, Portugal and Australia. Feral horses gather in groups of 3 to 20 animals and roam over large plains or on mountain foothills. A dominant stallion leads the group, which consists of mares and young foals. **693 dots**

Page 21

Icebergs of Antarctica

Made from fresh water, icebergs float around the sea off the coasts of the Arctic and Antarctica. Small icebergs weigh hundreds of tonnes; typical ones weigh 100,000 tonnes and the biggest ones can weigh billions of tonnes. They can look spectacularly beautiful, but are also very dangerous. The amount of ice that lurks below the sea level can vary from between 50 percent to 99 percent. **458 dots**

Page 22

Autumn Leaves

During the summer months deciduous leaves are bright green in colour due to the chemical chlorophyll (used in photosynthesis). During the winter months there is not enough light for photosynthesis to occur so the green chlorophyll disappears from the leaves, leaving the colours yellow and orange. Bright reds and purples are created as a result of trapped glucose being turned red by the last rays of the autumn sun. **809 dots**

Page 23

Lightning over Chicago

Lightning is a huge discharge of electricity. In a thundercloud, tiny drops of water and ice carry little bits of electricity, called electrical charges, which build up in parts of the cloud. In time, this charge becomes so great that electricity jumps to the ground or to other clouds, creating great sparks of lightning. Light travels so fast that we see a flash of lightning almost instantly. **258 dots**

Page 24

Mountain Bluebird

The feathers of a male mountain bluebird are a beautiful sky-blue, with the female being mostly grey-brown with tinges of pale blue in its wings and tail. Part of the family of thrushes, they nest in tree cavities and forage for insects such as beetles, grasshoppers, caterpillars and ants. During the winter months berries form an important part of their diet. The mountain bluebird is the state bird of Idaho and Nevada. **898 dots**

Page 25

Mountain Goat

This extremely agile creature is found across the Rocky Mountain and coastal ranges of northwestern North America. Despite its name, the mountain goat is a member of the antelope family and has a long face, long black horns and a short tail. It is often seen scaling steep, rocky ledges searching for grass, sedges, herbs, ferns and lichen upon which it feeds. **812 dots**

Page 26

Mouse

In the wild, mice are herbivores that eat a wide range of fruit and grains. They live in social groups building complex burrows with long entrances and many escape routes. They are mainly nocturnal creatures with poor eyesight, which they make up for by their keen hearing and strong sense of smell. They have many predators including cats, foxes, birds of prey and snakes. **855 dots**

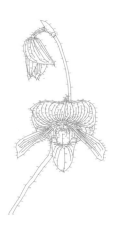

Page 27

Orchid

Flamboyant, intriguing, beautiful and exotic, orchids have evolved to become the largest family of plants in the world, and their diversity and distribution are virtually unchallenged in the plant kingdom. Every land habitat where it is possible for a plant to grow will contain orchids. They thrive on windswept mountain tops and in steaming tropical jungles. They also cling to niches in the bitterly cold Arctic regions and can endure the hottest, driest deserts. **556 dots**

Page 28

Tawny Owl

The distinctive double-call notes of these owls reveal their presence, even though their dark coloration makes them difficult to spot. Tawny owls prefer ancient woodland, where trees are large enough to provide hollow nesting cavities. Nocturnal by nature, these owls may nevertheless occasionally hunt during the daytime, particularly when they have chicks in the nest. **670 dots**

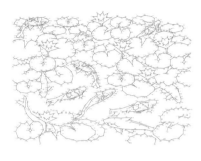

Page 29

Garden Pond

A garden pond is a much-loved feature of many gardens, adding light and movement. It attracts a wide range of wild creatures including frogs, toads, newts, dragonflies, mayflies, pond skaters and many more. Birds, too, love to bathe in the shallow areas at the edges of ponds. When adding fish to a pond it is important to have a balance of bottom, mid and surface feeders to ensure they are all doing their part in maintaining the pond's eco-system. **1286 dots**

Page 30

Poppies

This fragile, bright red wildflower brings a riot of summer vibrancy to farmers' fields and gardens alike. Mixed in with roses, lavenders and other perennials, poppies provide a romantic carefree look to a herbaceous border, or can be grown in pots as signature plants. They are very easy to grow from seed, and many of them re-seed to provide beauty for many years to come. **860 dots**

Page 31

Ram

Not to be confused with mountain goats, rams are male bighorn sheep that live in the mountains and can be identified by their long, curved horns, long fur and split hooves. They live in the Rocky Mountain region of North America in high outcrops. Thanks to their amazing balance, bighorn sheep can stand on ledges that are only 5cm/2in wide. They can also jump 6m/20ft and can run swiftly up a mountain to evade predators. **1041 dots**

Page 32

Roses

The rose is probably a native of the northern hemisphere and has been carried by settlers all over the world, where it has adapted and flourished. These beautiful plants come in a range of hues, many with scented blooms, and can be grown in herbaceous borders, in pots, and trained over arches and pergolas. They are easy to grow and, if looked after well, can live for many decades. **680 dots**

Page 33

Stag

In Britain, red deer are most common in the Scottish Highlands. In North America, ta related species is known as elk or wapiti. Their preferred habitat is large woodlands where they feed on grass, fruit, twigs and bark. Only male red deer have antlers, which can reach up to 1.7m/5.5ft across. The stags use their antlers during the rut to establish which male will control the harem of females. **602 dots**

Page 34

Sunflower

Native to North America but found around the world, the sunflower is both beautiful and useful. It is widely cultivated for its edible seeds and nutritious oil. As their name suggests, sunflower buds track the sun across the sky until the end of the bud cycle, when they finally position themselves facing due East. This makes sunflowers growing in the open a useful living compass, with north to the left, west behind and south to the right. **709 dots**

Page 35

Sunset in Hawaii

Hawaii is one of the most memorable places to watch the sun go down. Spellbinding red, orange, pink and blue hues leave spectators in awe as they watch these inspirational sunsets. At the time of sunset, more light is piercing the atmosphere than at other times during the day. The day's hot air has created a high number of air-born particles, which are able to scatter more light. The geography of Hawaii, tropical temperatures and humidity levels combine to give such a spectacular sunset experience. **463 dots**

Page 36

Tiger

The largest and most powerful of the cat family, the tiger's orange and black striped coat helps it to blend into dense undergrowth in tropical rainforest and mangrove swamp habitats in southwest Asia. Tigers are predominantly solitary creatures with groups consisting of a mother and her young. They lack the speed of other big cats, but their large and strong hind legs allow them to make surprisingly long leaps of up to 10m/33ft in length. **639 dots**

Page 37

Tornado

One of the most destructive forces in nature, tornadoes are born in violent thunderstorms. They appear when a funnel-shaped column of whirling air forms beneath a thundercloud and descends to the ground. With winds racing round at speeds of up to 500kph/300mph, a tornado destroys everything in its path, ripping houses to pieces and tossing cars into the air. Tornadoes occur regularly on the flat central plains of the USA, mostly along a line through Texas, Oklahoma, Kansas and Missouri; known locally as Tornado Alley. **397 dots**

Page 38

Volcano, Krakatoa

In August 1883, the volcano Krakatoa blasted itself apart with cataclysmic consequences. The ash clouds from the volcano rose high into the atmosphere, spreading out and moving in a band around the world. The explosion set off a devastating tsunami, which swept across the Indonesian island killing more than 36,000 people and destroying over two-thirds of the island. The explosion is considered to be the loudest sound ever heard in modern history. **441 dots**

Page 39

Water Lily and Dragon Fly

Dragonflies are large, active insects with compound eyes and a flexible neck. They can be seen patrolling the air over ponds and lakes, hovering every so often and chasing other insects for food. The larva lives for a year or two among water plants and hunts for other freshwater invertebrates, which it catches by means of its extendible 'mask', which it shoots out forward from the front of its face. **719 dots**

Page 40

Giant Puffballs

The giant puffball is a truly spectacular mushroom with a fruit body that can range from 5–80cm/2–31.5in across. It grows in gardens, pastures, woodlands and a wide variety of other situations, such as along stream banks. The season is any time from early summer to late autumn, unless the weather is very dry, when it will not grow. There will usually be several in the same area and they will continue to grow in the same spot year after year. **861 dots**

This edition published by Southwater,
an imprint of Anness Publishing Ltd,
108 Great Russell Street, London WC1B 3NA
www.annesspublishing.com; info@anness.com
Twitter: @Anness_Books

Publisher: Joanna Lorenz
Editorial Director: Helen Sudell
Illustrations by Glyn Bridgewater
Production Controller: Ben Worley

Publisher's Note
Although the information in this book is believed to be accurate and true at the time of going
to press neither the author nor the publisher can accept any legal responsibility for any errors
or ommissions that may have been made.